50 Premium Ham Recipes

By: Kelly Johnson

Table of Contents

- Honey-Glazed Ham
- Maple Mustard Glazed Ham
- Pineapple-Studded Baked Ham
- Herb-Crusted Ham
- Brown Sugar and Bourbon Glazed Ham
- Mustard and Brown Sugar Glazed Ham
- Garlic and Herb Roasted Ham
- Teriyaki Glazed Ham
- Cranberry Orange Glazed Ham
- Spiced Apple Cider Ham
- Coffee-Glazed Ham
- Chipotle Pineapple Glazed Ham
- Apricot-Glazed Ham
- Rosemary and Garlic Infused Ham
- Orange and Ginger Glazed Ham
- Southern-Style Glazed Ham
- Bourbon Maple Glazed Ham
- Glazed Ham with Pomegranate Molasses
- Jamaican Jerk Glazed Ham
- Honey and Thyme Glazed Ham
- Mustard and Maple Glazed Ham
- Cherry-Glazed Ham
- Ham with Dijon and Herb Crust
- Savory Glazed Ham with Thyme
- Cider Vinegar and Brown Sugar Ham
- Beer-Braised Ham
- Maple-Glazed Ham with Walnuts
- Honey-Bourbon Glazed Ham
- Hoisin and Ginger Glazed Ham
- Smoked Paprika Glazed Ham
- Brown Sugar and Soy Sauce Glazed Ham
- Pecan-Crusted Ham
- Maple-Rum Glazed Ham
- Garlic Parmesan Crusted Ham
- Spicy Honey Glazed Ham

- Apricot-Mustard Glazed Ham
- Sweet and Spicy Glazed Ham
- Zesty Citrus Glazed Ham
- Maple-Sriracha Glazed Ham
- Soy-Ginger Glazed Ham
- Balsamic Vinegar Glazed Ham
- Honey-Chipotle Glazed Ham
- Sweet and Tangy Glazed Ham
- Red Pepper Jelly Glazed Ham
- Maple-Cranberry Glazed Ham
- Citrus and Herb Marinated Ham
- Honey-Cider Glazed Ham
- Blackberry Glazed Ham
- Garlic and Honey Glazed Ham
- Lemon-Herb Glazed Ham

Honey-Glazed Ham

Ingredients:

- 1 fully cooked bone-in ham (about 8-10 pounds)
- 1 cup honey
- 1/2 cup brown sugar
- 1/4 cup Dijon mustard
- 1/4 cup apple cider vinegar
- 1 teaspoon ground cinnamon
- 1/2 teaspoon ground cloves
- 1/2 teaspoon ground ginger

Instructions:

1. Preheat the Oven: Preheat your oven to 325°F (165°C).
2. Prepare the Ham: Score the surface of the ham in a diamond pattern, making shallow cuts about 1 inch apart. Place the ham in a roasting pan, cut side down.
3. Make the Glaze: In a saucepan, combine honey, brown sugar, Dijon mustard, apple cider vinegar, cinnamon, cloves, and ginger. Heat over medium heat, stirring until the sugar is dissolved and the mixture is smooth.
4. Glaze the Ham: Brush the ham generously with the glaze, reserving some for basting.
5. Bake the Ham: Cover the ham with aluminum foil and bake for about 1 hour. Remove the foil and brush with more glaze. Continue baking for an additional 30 minutes, basting every 10 minutes, until heated through and caramelized.
6. Serve: Let the ham rest for 15 minutes before slicing and serving.

Maple Mustard Glazed Ham

Ingredients:

- 1 fully cooked bone-in ham (about 8-10 pounds)
- 1 cup pure maple syrup
- 1/4 cup Dijon mustard
- 1/4 cup brown sugar
- 2 tablespoons apple cider vinegar
- 1 teaspoon ground black pepper
- 1/2 teaspoon ground allspice

Instructions:

1. Preheat the Oven: Preheat your oven to 325°F (165°C).
2. Prepare the Ham: Score the surface of the ham in a diamond pattern, making shallow cuts about 1 inch apart. Place the ham in a roasting pan, cut side down.
3. Make the Glaze: In a mixing bowl, whisk together maple syrup, Dijon mustard, brown sugar, apple cider vinegar, black pepper, and allspice until well combined.
4. Glaze the Ham: Brush the ham generously with the maple mustard glaze, reserving some for basting.
5. Bake the Ham: Cover the ham with aluminum foil and bake for about 1 hour. Remove the foil and brush with more glaze. Continue baking for an additional 30 minutes, basting every 10 minutes, until heated through and nicely caramelized.
6. Serve: Allow the ham to rest for 15 minutes before slicing and serving.

Pineapple-Studded Baked Ham

Ingredients:

- 1 fully cooked bone-in ham (6-8 lbs)
- 1 cup brown sugar
- 1/2 cup honey
- 1 can sliced pineapple (in juice)
- Whole cloves (optional)

Instructions:

1. **Preheat Oven:** Preheat your oven to 325°F (163°C).
2. **Prepare Ham:** Score the surface of the ham in a diamond pattern and place it in a roasting pan, cut side down.
3. **Make Glaze:** In a bowl, mix brown sugar and honey until well combined. Spread this mixture over the ham.
4. **Add Pineapple:** Arrange the pineapple slices on the ham, securing them with whole cloves if desired.
5. **Bake:** Cover the ham loosely with foil and bake for about 1.5 to 2 hours, basting with the juices every 30 minutes.
6. **Serve:** Let the ham rest for 15 minutes before slicing. Serve warm.

Herb-Crusted Ham

Ingredients:

- 1 fully cooked boneless ham (4-6 lbs)
- 1/4 cup Dijon mustard
- 1/4 cup honey
- 1 tablespoon fresh rosemary, chopped
- 1 tablespoon fresh thyme, chopped
- 1 teaspoon garlic powder
- Salt and pepper to taste

Instructions:

1. **Preheat Oven:** Preheat your oven to 325°F (163°C).
2. **Prepare Ham:** Place the ham in a roasting pan.
3. **Make Herb Mixture:** In a bowl, combine Dijon mustard, honey, rosemary, thyme, garlic powder, salt, and pepper.
4. **Coat Ham:** Brush the herb mixture all over the ham.
5. **Bake:** Cover the ham loosely with foil and bake for 1.5 to 2 hours, basting occasionally.
6. **Serve:** Allow the ham to rest for 10-15 minutes before slicing. Enjoy warm.

Brown Sugar and Bourbon Glazed Ham

Ingredients:

- 1 fully cooked bone-in ham (6-8 lbs)
- 1 cup brown sugar
- 1/2 cup bourbon
- 1/4 cup Dijon mustard
- 1/4 teaspoon ground cloves

Instructions:

1. **Preheat Oven:** Preheat your oven to 325°F (163°C).
2. **Prepare Ham:** Score the surface of the ham and place it in a roasting pan.
3. **Make Glaze:** In a saucepan, combine brown sugar, bourbon, Dijon mustard, and ground cloves. Heat until the sugar dissolves.
4. **Glaze Ham:** Brush the glaze over the ham.
5. **Bake:** Cover loosely with foil and bake for 1.5 to 2 hours, basting every 30 minutes.
6. **Serve:** Let the ham rest for 15 minutes before slicing. Serve warm.

Mustard and Brown Sugar Glazed Ham

Ingredients:

- 1 fully cooked boneless ham (4-6 lbs)
- 1/2 cup brown sugar
- 1/4 cup Dijon mustard
- 1/4 teaspoon ground black pepper

Instructions:

1. **Preheat Oven:** Preheat your oven to 325°F (163°C).
2. **Prepare Ham:** Place the ham in a roasting pan.
3. **Make Glaze:** In a bowl, mix brown sugar, Dijon mustard, and black pepper until smooth.
4. **Coat Ham:** Brush the glaze over the surface of the ham.
5. **Bake:** Cover loosely with foil and bake for 1.5 to 2 hours, basting occasionally.
6. **Serve:** Allow to rest for 10-15 minutes before slicing. Enjoy warm.

Garlic and Herb Roasted Ham

Ingredients:

- 1 fully cooked bone-in ham (6-8 lbs)
- 1/4 cup olive oil
- 4 cloves garlic, minced
- 2 tablespoons fresh thyme, chopped
- 2 tablespoons fresh rosemary, chopped
- Salt and pepper to taste

Instructions:

1. **Preheat Oven:** Preheat your oven to 325°F (163°C).
2. **Prepare Ham:** Score the surface of the ham and place it in a roasting pan.
3. **Make Garlic Herb Mixture:** In a bowl, mix olive oil, minced garlic, thyme, rosemary, salt, and pepper.
4. **Coat Ham:** Rub the mixture all over the ham.
5. **Bake:** Cover loosely with foil and bake for 1.5 to 2 hours, basting every 30 minutes.
6. **Serve:** Let the ham rest for 10-15 minutes before slicing. Serve warm.

Teriyaki Glazed Ham

Ingredients:

- 1 fully cooked boneless ham (4-6 lbs)
- 1 cup teriyaki sauce
- 1/2 cup brown sugar
- 1/4 cup pineapple juice
- 1 tablespoon sesame seeds (optional)

Instructions:

1. **Preheat Oven:** Preheat your oven to 325°F (163°C).
2. **Prepare Ham:** Place the ham in a roasting pan.
3. **Make Teriyaki Glaze:** In a saucepan, combine teriyaki sauce, brown sugar, and pineapple juice. Heat until the sugar dissolves.
4. **Glaze Ham:** Brush half of the glaze over the ham.
5. **Bake:** Cover loosely with foil and bake for 1.5 to 2 hours, basting with the remaining glaze every 30 minutes.
6. **Serve:** Allow the ham to rest for 10-15 minutes before slicing. Sprinkle with sesame seeds if desired.

Cranberry Orange Glazed Ham

Ingredients:

- 1 fully cooked bone-in ham (6-8 lbs)
- 1 cup cranberry sauce
- 1/2 cup orange juice
- 1/4 cup brown sugar
- 1 teaspoon ground cinnamon

Instructions:

1. **Preheat Oven:** Preheat your oven to 325°F (163°C).
2. **Prepare Ham:** Score the surface of the ham and place it in a roasting pan.
3. **Make Glaze:** In a bowl, mix cranberry sauce, orange juice, brown sugar, and cinnamon until smooth.
4. **Glaze Ham:** Brush the glaze over the ham.
5. **Bake:** Cover loosely with foil and bake for 1.5 to 2 hours, basting every 30 minutes.
6. **Serve:** Let the ham rest for 15 minutes before slicing. Enjoy warm.

Spiced Apple Cider Ham

Ingredients:

- 1 fully cooked boneless ham (4-6 lbs)
- 1 cup apple cider
- 1/2 cup brown sugar
- 1 tablespoon Dijon mustard
- 1 teaspoon ground nutmeg
- 1 teaspoon ground cloves

Instructions:

1. **Preheat Oven:** Preheat your oven to 325°F (163°C).
2. **Prepare Ham:** Place the ham in a roasting pan.
3. **Make Glaze:** In a saucepan, combine apple cider, brown sugar, Dijon mustard, nutmeg, and cloves. Heat until the sugar dissolves.
4. **Glaze Ham:** Brush the mixture over the ham.
5. **Bake:** Cover loosely with foil and bake for 1.5 to 2 hours, basting every 30 minutes.
6. **Serve:** Allow the ham to rest for 10-15 minutes before slicing. Enjoy warm.

Coffee-Glazed Ham

Ingredients:

- 1 fully cooked bone-in ham (6-8 lbs)
- 1 cup brewed coffee
- 1/2 cup brown sugar
- 1/4 cup maple syrup
- 1 tablespoon Dijon mustard

Instructions:

1. **Preheat Oven:** Preheat your oven to 325°F (163°C).
2. **Prepare Ham:** Score the surface of the ham and place it in a roasting pan.
3. **Make Glaze:** In a saucepan, combine brewed coffee, brown sugar, maple syrup, and Dijon mustard. Heat until combined.
4. **Glaze Ham:** Brush the coffee glaze over the ham.
5. **Bake:** Cover loosely with foil and bake for 1.5 to 2 hours, basting every 30 minutes.
6. **Serve:** Let the ham rest for 15 minutes before slicing. Enjoy warm.

Chipotle Pineapple Glazed Ham

Ingredients:

- 1 fully cooked boneless ham (4-6 lbs)
- 1 cup pineapple juice
- 1/2 cup brown sugar
- 2-3 chipotle peppers in adobo sauce, minced
- 1 tablespoon Dijon mustard

Instructions:

1. **Preheat Oven:** Preheat your oven to 325°F (163°C).
2. **Prepare Ham:** Place the ham in a roasting pan.
3. **Make Glaze:** In a saucepan, combine pineapple juice, brown sugar, minced chipotle peppers, and Dijon mustard. Heat until smooth.
4. **Glaze Ham:** Brush the glaze over the ham.
5. **Bake:** Cover loosely with foil and bake for 1.5 to 2 hours, basting every 30 minutes.
6. **Serve:** Allow the ham to rest for 10-15 minutes before slicing. Enjoy warm.

Apricot-Glazed Ham

Ingredients:

- 1 fully cooked bone-in ham (6-8 lbs)
- 1 cup apricot preserves
- 1/4 cup Dijon mustard
- 1/4 teaspoon ground ginger

Instructions:

1. **Preheat Oven:** Preheat your oven to 325°F (163°C).
2. **Prepare Ham:** Score the surface of the ham and place it in a roasting pan.
3. **Make Glaze:** In a bowl, mix apricot preserves, Dijon mustard, and ground ginger until smooth.
4. **Glaze Ham:** Brush the glaze over the ham.
5. **Bake:** Cover loosely with foil and bake for 1.5 to 2 hours, basting every 30 minutes.
6. **Serve:** Let the ham rest for 15 minutes before slicing. Enjoy warm.

Rosemary and Garlic Infused Ham

Ingredients:

- 1 fully cooked boneless ham (4-6 lbs)
- 1/4 cup olive oil
- 4 cloves garlic, minced
- 2 tablespoons fresh rosemary, chopped
- Salt and pepper to taste

Instructions:

1. **Preheat Oven:** Preheat your oven to 325°F (163°C).
2. **Prepare Ham:** Score the surface of the ham and place it in a roasting pan.
3. **Make Infusion:** In a bowl, mix olive oil, minced garlic, rosemary, salt, and pepper.
4. **Coat Ham:** Rub the mixture all over the ham.
5. **Bake:** Cover loosely with foil and bake for 1.5 to 2 hours, basting every 30 minutes.
6. **Serve:** Allow the ham to rest for 10-15 minutes before slicing. Enjoy warm.

Orange and Ginger Glazed Ham

Ingredients:

- 1 fully cooked bone-in ham (6-8 lbs)
- 1 cup orange marmalade
- 1/4 cup ginger ale
- 1 tablespoon Dijon mustard

Instructions:

1. **Preheat Oven:** Preheat your oven to 325°F (163°C).
2. **Prepare Ham:** Score the surface of the ham and place it in a roasting pan.
3. **Make Glaze:** In a bowl, mix orange marmalade, ginger ale, and Dijon mustard until well combined.
4. **Glaze Ham:** Brush the glaze over the ham.
5. **Bake:** Cover loosely with foil and bake for 1.5 to 2 hours, basting every 30 minutes.
6. **Serve:** Let the ham rest for 15 minutes before slicing. Enjoy warm.

Southern-Style Glazed Ham

Ingredients:

- 1 fully cooked boneless ham (4-6 lbs)
- 1 cup cola
- 1/2 cup brown sugar
- 1/4 cup Dijon mustard
- 1 teaspoon ground black pepper

Instructions:

1. **Preheat Oven:** Preheat your oven to 325°F (163°C).
2. **Prepare Ham:** Place the ham in a roasting pan.
3. **Make Glaze:** In a saucepan, combine cola, brown sugar, Dijon mustard, and black pepper. Heat until the sugar dissolves.
4. **Glaze Ham:** Brush the mixture over the ham.
5. **Bake:** Cover loosely with foil and bake for 1.5 to 2 hours, basting every 30 minutes.
6. **Serve:** Allow the ham to rest for 10-15 minutes before slicing. Enjoy warm.

Bourbon Maple Glazed Ham

Ingredients:

- 1 fully cooked bone-in ham (6-8 lbs)
- 1 cup maple syrup
- 1/2 cup bourbon
- 1/4 cup brown sugar
- 1 tablespoon Dijon mustard

Instructions:

1. **Preheat Oven:** Preheat your oven to 325°F (163°C).
2. **Prepare Ham:** Score the surface of the ham and place it in a roasting pan.
3. **Make Glaze:** In a saucepan, combine maple syrup, bourbon, brown sugar, and Dijon mustard. Heat until combined.
4. **Glaze Ham:** Brush the glaze over the ham.
5. **Bake:** Cover loosely with foil and bake for 1.5 to 2 hours, basting every 30 minutes.
6. **Serve:** Let the ham rest for 15 minutes before slicing. Enjoy warm.

Glazed Ham with Pomegranate Molasses

Ingredients:

- 1 fully cooked boneless ham (4-6 lbs)
- 1/2 cup pomegranate molasses
- 1/4 cup honey
- 1 tablespoon Dijon mustard
- 1 teaspoon ground cinnamon

Instructions:

1. **Preheat Oven:** Preheat your oven to 325°F (163°C).
2. **Prepare Ham:** Place the ham in a roasting pan.
3. **Make Glaze:** In a bowl, mix pomegranate molasses, honey, Dijon mustard, and cinnamon until smooth.
4. **Glaze Ham:** Brush the mixture over the ham.
5. **Bake:** Cover loosely with foil and bake for 1.5 to 2 hours, basting every 30 minutes.
6. **Serve:** Allow the ham to rest for 10-15 minutes before slicing. Enjoy warm.

Jamaican Jerk Glazed Ham

Ingredients:

- 1 fully cooked bone-in ham (6-8 lbs)
- 1/4 cup jerk seasoning
- 1/2 cup orange juice
- 1/4 cup brown sugar
- 2 tablespoons honey

Instructions:

1. **Preheat Oven:** Preheat your oven to 325°F (163°C).
2. **Prepare Ham:** Score the surface of the ham and place it in a roasting pan.
3. **Make Glaze:** In a bowl, mix jerk seasoning, orange juice, brown sugar, and honey until well combined.
4. **Glaze Ham:** Brush the mixture over the ham.
5. **Bake:** Cover loosely with foil and bake for 1.5 to 2 hours, basting every 30 minutes.
6. **Serve:** Let the ham rest for 15 minutes before slicing. Enjoy warm.

Honey and Thyme Glazed Ham

Ingredients:

- 1 fully cooked boneless ham (4-6 lbs)
- 1/2 cup honey
- 2 tablespoons fresh thyme, chopped
- 1 tablespoon Dijon mustard
- Salt and pepper to taste

Instructions:

1. **Preheat Oven:** Preheat your oven to 325°F (163°C).
2. **Prepare Ham:** Place the ham in a roasting pan.
3. **Make Glaze:** In a bowl, mix honey, thyme, Dijon mustard, salt, and pepper until combined.
4. **Glaze Ham:** Brush the mixture over the ham.
5. **Bake:** Cover loosely with foil and bake for 1.5 to 2 hours, basting every 30 minutes.
6. **Serve:** Allow the ham to rest for 10-15 minutes before slicing. Enjoy warm.

Mustard and Maple Glazed Ham

Ingredients:

- 1 fully cooked bone-in ham (6-8 lbs)
- 1/2 cup maple syrup
- 1/4 cup Dijon mustard
- 1/4 cup brown sugar
- 1 teaspoon black pepper

Instructions:

1. **Preheat Oven:** Preheat your oven to 325°F (163°C).
2. **Prepare Ham:** Score the surface of the ham and place it in a roasting pan.
3. **Make Glaze:** In a bowl, mix maple syrup, Dijon mustard, brown sugar, and black pepper until smooth.
4. **Glaze Ham:** Brush the mixture over the ham.
5. **Bake:** Cover loosely with foil and bake for 1.5 to 2 hours, basting every 30 minutes.
6. **Serve:** Let the ham rest for 15 minutes before slicing. Enjoy warm.

Cherry-Glazed Ham

Ingredients:

- 1 fully cooked boneless ham (4-6 lbs)
- 1 cup cherry preserves
- 1/4 cup red wine vinegar
- 1 tablespoon Dijon mustard
- 1 teaspoon ground cloves

Instructions:

1. **Preheat Oven:** Preheat your oven to 325°F (163°C).
2. **Prepare Ham:** Place the ham in a roasting pan.
3. **Make Glaze:** In a saucepan, combine cherry preserves, red wine vinegar, Dijon mustard, and ground cloves. Heat until smooth.
4. **Glaze Ham:** Brush the glaze over the ham.
5. **Bake:** Cover loosely with foil and bake for 1.5 to 2 hours, basting every 30 minutes.
6. **Serve:** Allow the ham to rest for 10-15 minutes before slicing. Enjoy warm.

Ham with Dijon and Herb Crust

Ingredients:

- 1 fully cooked bone-in ham (6-8 lbs)
- 1/2 cup Dijon mustard
- 1/4 cup breadcrumbs
- 2 tablespoons fresh herbs (thyme, rosemary, or parsley), chopped
- Salt and pepper to taste

Instructions:

1. **Preheat Oven:** Preheat your oven to 325°F (163°C).
2. **Prepare Ham:** Score the surface of the ham and place it in a roasting pan.
3. **Make Crust:** In a bowl, mix Dijon mustard, breadcrumbs, herbs, salt, and pepper until combined.
4. **Coat Ham:** Spread the mixture over the top of the ham.
5. **Bake:** Cover loosely with foil and bake for 1.5 to 2 hours, basting every 30 minutes.
6. **Serve:** Let the ham rest for 15 minutes before slicing. Enjoy warm.

Savory Glazed Ham with Thyme

Ingredients:

- 1 fully cooked boneless ham (4-6 lbs)
- 1/2 cup honey
- 1/4 cup balsamic vinegar
- 2 tablespoons fresh thyme, chopped
- 1 tablespoon Dijon mustard

Instructions:

1. **Preheat Oven:** Preheat your oven to 325°F (163°C).
2. **Prepare Ham:** Place the ham in a roasting pan.
3. **Make Glaze:** In a bowl, mix honey, balsamic vinegar, thyme, and Dijon mustard until smooth.
4. **Glaze Ham:** Brush the mixture over the ham.
5. **Bake:** Cover loosely with foil and bake for 1.5 to 2 hours, basting every 30 minutes.
6. **Serve:** Allow the ham to rest for 10-15 minutes before slicing. Enjoy warm.

Cider Vinegar and Brown Sugar Ham

Ingredients:

- 1 fully cooked bone-in ham (6-8 lbs)
- 1/2 cup brown sugar
- 1/4 cup cider vinegar
- 1 tablespoon Dijon mustard
- 1 teaspoon ground cinnamon

Instructions:

1. **Preheat Oven:** Preheat your oven to 325°F (163°C).
2. **Prepare Ham:** Score the surface of the ham and place it in a roasting pan.
3. **Make Glaze:** In a bowl, mix brown sugar, cider vinegar, Dijon mustard, and cinnamon until smooth.
4. **Glaze Ham:** Brush the mixture over the ham.
5. **Bake:** Cover loosely with foil and bake for 1.5 to 2 hours, basting every 30 minutes.
6. **Serve:** Allow the ham to rest for 15 minutes before slicing. Enjoy warm.

Beer-Braised Ham

Ingredients:

- 1 fully cooked bone-in ham (6-8 lbs)
- 1 can (12 oz) beer (lager or ale)
- 1/2 cup brown sugar
- 1/4 cup Dijon mustard
- 1 tablespoon Worcestershire sauce

Instructions:

1. **Preheat Oven:** Preheat your oven to 325°F (163°C).
2. **Prepare Ham:** Score the surface of the ham and place it in a roasting pan.
3. **Make Braise:** In a bowl, mix beer, brown sugar, Dijon mustard, and Worcestershire sauce until well combined.
4. **Braised Ham:** Pour the mixture over the ham.
5. **Bake:** Cover loosely with foil and bake for 1.5 to 2 hours, basting every 30 minutes.
6. **Serve:** Let the ham rest for 15 minutes before slicing. Enjoy warm.

Maple-Glazed Ham with Walnuts

Ingredients:

- 1 fully cooked boneless ham (4-6 lbs)
- 1 cup maple syrup
- 1/2 cup walnuts, chopped
- 1/4 cup brown sugar
- 1 tablespoon Dijon mustard

Instructions:

1. **Preheat Oven:** Preheat your oven to 325°F (163°C).
2. **Prepare Ham:** Place the ham in a roasting pan.
3. **Make Glaze:** In a saucepan, combine maple syrup, walnuts, brown sugar, and Dijon mustard. Heat until smooth.
4. **Glaze Ham:** Brush the mixture over the ham.
5. **Bake:** Cover loosely with foil and bake for 1.5 to 2 hours, basting every 30 minutes.
6. **Serve:** Allow the ham to rest for 10-15 minutes before slicing. Enjoy warm.

Honey-Bourbon Glazed Ham

Ingredients:

- 1 fully cooked bone-in ham (6-8 lbs)
- 1/2 cup honey
- 1/4 cup bourbon
- 1/4 cup brown sugar
- 1 tablespoon Dijon mustard

Instructions:

1. **Preheat Oven:** Preheat your oven to 325°F (163°C).
2. **Prepare Ham:** Score the surface of the ham and place it in a roasting pan.
3. **Make Glaze:** In a bowl, mix honey, bourbon, brown sugar, and Dijon mustard until well combined.
4. **Glaze Ham:** Brush the mixture over the ham.
5. **Bake:** Cover loosely with foil and bake for 1.5 to 2 hours, basting every 30 minutes.
6. **Serve:** Let the ham rest for 15 minutes before slicing. Enjoy warm.

Hoisin and Ginger Glazed Ham

Ingredients:

- 1 fully cooked boneless ham (4-6 lbs)
- 1/2 cup hoisin sauce
- 1/4 cup fresh ginger, grated
- 1/4 cup brown sugar
- 1 tablespoon soy sauce

Instructions:

1. **Preheat Oven:** Preheat your oven to 325°F (163°C).
2. **Prepare Ham:** Place the ham in a roasting pan.
3. **Make Glaze:** In a bowl, mix hoisin sauce, ginger, brown sugar, and soy sauce until smooth.
4. **Glaze Ham:** Brush the mixture over the ham.
5. **Bake:** Cover loosely with foil and bake for 1.5 to 2 hours, basting every 30 minutes.
6. **Serve:** Allow the ham to rest for 10-15 minutes before slicing. Enjoy warm.

Smoked Paprika Glazed Ham

Ingredients:

- 1 fully cooked bone-in ham (6-8 lbs)
- 1/2 cup brown sugar
- 1/4 cup apple cider vinegar
- 1 tablespoon smoked paprika
- 1 teaspoon cayenne pepper (optional)

Instructions:

1. **Preheat Oven:** Preheat your oven to 325°F (163°C).
2. **Prepare Ham:** Score the surface of the ham and place it in a roasting pan.
3. **Make Glaze:** In a bowl, mix brown sugar, apple cider vinegar, smoked paprika, and cayenne pepper until smooth.
4. **Glaze Ham:** Brush the mixture over the ham.
5. **Bake:** Cover loosely with foil and bake for 1.5 to 2 hours, basting every 30 minutes.
6. **Serve:** Let the ham rest for 15 minutes before slicing. Enjoy warm.

Brown Sugar and Soy Sauce Glazed Ham

Ingredients:

- 1 fully cooked boneless ham (4-6 lbs)
- 1/2 cup brown sugar
- 1/4 cup soy sauce
- 1/4 cup apple cider vinegar
- 1 tablespoon ginger, minced

Instructions:

1. **Preheat Oven:** Preheat your oven to 325°F (163°C).
2. **Prepare Ham:** Place the ham in a roasting pan.
3. **Make Glaze:** In a bowl, mix brown sugar, soy sauce, apple cider vinegar, and minced ginger until well combined.
4. **Glaze Ham:** Brush the mixture over the ham.
5. **Bake:** Cover loosely with foil and bake for 1.5 to 2 hours, basting every 30 minutes.
6. **Serve:** Allow the ham to rest for 10-15 minutes before slicing. Enjoy warm.

Pecan-Crusted Ham

Ingredients:

- 1 fully cooked bone-in ham (6-8 lbs)
- 1 cup pecans, finely chopped
- 1/2 cup brown sugar
- 1/4 cup Dijon mustard
- 1 tablespoon maple syrup

Instructions:

1. **Preheat Oven:** Preheat your oven to 325°F (163°C).
2. **Prepare Ham:** Score the surface of the ham and place it in a roasting pan.
3. **Make Crust:** In a bowl, mix pecans, brown sugar, Dijon mustard, and maple syrup until combined.
4. **Coat Ham:** Spread the mixture over the top of the ham.
5. **Bake:** Cover loosely with foil and bake for 1.5 to 2 hours, basting every 30 minutes.
6. **Serve:** Let the ham rest for 15 minutes before slicing. Enjoy warm.

Maple-Rum Glazed Ham

Ingredients:

- 1 fully cooked bone-in ham (6-8 lbs)
- 1/2 cup maple syrup
- 1/4 cup dark rum
- 1/4 cup brown sugar
- 1 tablespoon Dijon mustard

Instructions:

1. **Preheat Oven:** Preheat your oven to 325°F (163°C).
2. **Prepare Ham:** Score the surface of the ham and place it in a roasting pan.
3. **Make Glaze:** In a bowl, mix maple syrup, dark rum, brown sugar, and Dijon mustard until smooth.
4. **Glaze Ham:** Brush the mixture over the ham.
5. **Bake:** Cover loosely with foil and bake for 1.5 to 2 hours, basting every 30 minutes.
6. **Serve:** Allow the ham to rest for 15 minutes before slicing. Enjoy warm.

Garlic Parmesan Crusted Ham

Ingredients:

- 1 fully cooked bone-in ham (6-8 lbs)
- 1/2 cup grated Parmesan cheese
- 1/4 cup breadcrumbs
- 3 cloves garlic, minced
- 1 tablespoon olive oil
- 1 teaspoon dried oregano

Instructions:

1. **Preheat Oven:** Preheat your oven to 325°F (163°C).
2. **Prepare Ham:** Score the surface of the ham and place it in a roasting pan.
3. **Make Crust:** In a bowl, combine Parmesan cheese, breadcrumbs, minced garlic, olive oil, and oregano.
4. **Coat Ham:** Spread the mixture over the top of the ham, pressing down gently to adhere.
5. **Bake:** Cover loosely with foil and bake for 1.5 to 2 hours, basting every 30 minutes.
6. **Serve:** Let the ham rest for 15 minutes before slicing. Enjoy warm.

Spicy Honey Glazed Ham

Ingredients:

- 1 fully cooked bone-in ham (6-8 lbs)
- 1/2 cup honey
- 1/4 cup sriracha sauce
- 1/4 cup brown sugar
- 1 tablespoon apple cider vinegar

Instructions:

1. **Preheat Oven:** Preheat your oven to 325°F (163°C).
2. **Prepare Ham:** Score the surface of the ham and place it in a roasting pan.
3. **Make Glaze:** In a bowl, mix honey, sriracha, brown sugar, and apple cider vinegar until smooth.
4. **Glaze Ham:** Brush the mixture over the ham.
5. **Bake:** Cover loosely with foil and bake for 1.5 to 2 hours, basting every 30 minutes.
6. **Serve:** Allow the ham to rest for 15 minutes before slicing. Enjoy warm.

Apricot-Mustard Glazed Ham

Ingredients:

- 1 fully cooked bone-in ham (6-8 lbs)
- 1/2 cup apricot preserves
- 1/4 cup Dijon mustard
- 1/4 cup brown sugar
- 1 tablespoon apple cider vinegar

Instructions:

1. **Preheat Oven:** Preheat your oven to 325°F (163°C).
2. **Prepare Ham:** Score the surface of the ham and place it in a roasting pan.
3. **Make Glaze:** In a bowl, mix apricot preserves, Dijon mustard, brown sugar, and apple cider vinegar until well combined.
4. **Glaze Ham:** Brush the mixture over the ham.
5. **Bake:** Cover loosely with foil and bake for 1.5 to 2 hours, basting every 30 minutes.
6. **Serve:** Let the ham rest for 15 minutes before slicing. Enjoy warm.

Sweet and Spicy Glazed Ham

Ingredients:

- 1 fully cooked bone-in ham (6-8 lbs)
- 1/2 cup brown sugar
- 1/4 cup honey
- 1/4 cup apple cider vinegar
- 2 tablespoons hot sauce

Instructions:

1. **Preheat Oven:** Preheat your oven to 325°F (163°C).
2. **Prepare Ham:** Score the surface of the ham and place it in a roasting pan.
3. **Make Glaze:** In a bowl, mix brown sugar, honey, apple cider vinegar, and hot sauce until smooth.
4. **Glaze Ham:** Brush the mixture over the ham.
5. **Bake:** Cover loosely with foil and bake for 1.5 to 2 hours, basting every 30 minutes.
6. **Serve:** Allow the ham to rest for 15 minutes before slicing. Enjoy warm.

Zesty Citrus Glazed Ham

Ingredients:

- 1 fully cooked bone-in ham (6-8 lbs)
- 1/2 cup orange juice
- 1/4 cup honey
- 1/4 cup Dijon mustard
- 1 tablespoon lemon zest

Instructions:

1. **Preheat Oven:** Preheat your oven to 325°F (163°C).
2. **Prepare Ham:** Score the surface of the ham and place it in a roasting pan.
3. **Make Glaze:** In a bowl, mix orange juice, honey, Dijon mustard, and lemon zest until smooth.
4. **Glaze Ham:** Brush the mixture over the ham.
5. **Bake:** Cover loosely with foil and bake for 1.5 to 2 hours, basting every 30 minutes.
6. **Serve:** Let the ham rest for 15 minutes before slicing. Enjoy warm.

Maple-Sriracha Glazed Ham

Ingredients:

- 1 fully cooked bone-in ham (6-8 lbs)
- 1/2 cup maple syrup
- 1/4 cup sriracha sauce
- 1/4 cup soy sauce
- 1 tablespoon apple cider vinegar

Instructions:

1. **Preheat Oven:** Preheat your oven to 325°F (163°C).
2. **Prepare Ham:** Score the surface of the ham and place it in a roasting pan.
3. **Make Glaze:** In a bowl, mix maple syrup, sriracha, soy sauce, and apple cider vinegar until well combined.
4. **Glaze Ham:** Brush the mixture over the ham.
5. **Bake:** Cover loosely with foil and bake for 1.5 to 2 hours, basting every 30 minutes.
6. **Serve:** Allow the ham to rest for 15 minutes before slicing. Enjoy warm.

Soy-Ginger Glazed Ham

Ingredients:

- 1 fully cooked bone-in ham (6-8 lbs)
- 1/2 cup soy sauce
- 1/4 cup honey
- 1/4 cup fresh ginger, grated
- 1 tablespoon sesame oil

Instructions:

1. **Preheat Oven:** Preheat your oven to 325°F (163°C).
2. **Prepare Ham:** Score the surface of the ham and place it in a roasting pan.
3. **Make Glaze:** In a bowl, mix soy sauce, honey, grated ginger, and sesame oil until well combined.
4. **Glaze Ham:** Brush the mixture over the ham.
5. **Bake:** Cover loosely with foil and bake for 1.5 to 2 hours, basting every 30 minutes.
6. **Serve:** Let the ham rest for 15 minutes before slicing. Enjoy warm.

Balsamic Vinegar Glazed Ham

Ingredients:

- 1 fully cooked bone-in ham (6-8 lbs)
- 1/2 cup balsamic vinegar
- 1/4 cup honey
- 1/4 cup brown sugar
- 1 tablespoon Dijon mustard

Instructions:

1. **Preheat Oven:** Preheat your oven to 325°F (163°C).
2. **Prepare Ham:** Score the surface of the ham and place it in a roasting pan.
3. **Make Glaze:** In a bowl, mix balsamic vinegar, honey, brown sugar, and Dijon mustard until smooth.
4. **Glaze Ham:** Brush the mixture over the ham.
5. **Bake:** Cover loosely with foil and bake for 1.5 to 2 hours, basting every 30 minutes.
6. **Serve:** Allow the ham to rest for 15 minutes before slicing. Enjoy warm.

Honey-Chipotle Glazed Ham

Ingredients:

- 1 fully cooked bone-in ham (6-8 lbs)
- 1/2 cup honey
- 1-2 tablespoons chipotle sauce (adjust for spice level)
- 1/4 cup brown sugar
- 1 tablespoon apple cider vinegar

Instructions:

1. **Preheat Oven:** Preheat your oven to 325°F (163°C).
2. **Prepare Ham:** Score the surface of the ham and place it in a roasting pan.
3. **Make Glaze:** In a bowl, mix honey, chipotle sauce, brown sugar, and apple cider vinegar until well combined.
4. **Glaze Ham:** Brush the mixture over the ham.
5. **Bake:** Cover loosely with foil and bake for 1.5 to 2 hours, basting every 30 minutes.
6. **Serve:** Let the ham rest for 15 minutes before slicing. Enjoy warm.

Sweet and Tangy Glazed Ham

Ingredients:

- 1 fully cooked bone-in ham (6-8 lbs)
- 1/2 cup brown sugar
- 1/4 cup apple cider vinegar
- 1/4 cup Dijon mustard
- 1 tablespoon Worcestershire sauce

Instructions:

1. **Preheat Oven:** Preheat your oven to 325°F (163°C).
2. **Prepare Ham:** Score the surface of the ham and place it in a roasting pan.
3. **Make Glaze:** In a bowl, mix brown sugar, apple cider vinegar, Dijon mustard, and Worcestershire sauce until smooth.
4. **Glaze Ham:** Brush the mixture over the ham.
5. **Bake:** Cover loosely with foil and bake for 1.5 to 2 hours, basting every 30 minutes.
6. **Serve:** Allow the ham to rest for 15 minutes before slicing. Enjoy warm.

Red Pepper Jelly Glazed Ham

Ingredients:

- 1 fully cooked bone-in ham (6-8 lbs)
- 1/2 cup red pepper jelly
- 1/4 cup Dijon mustard
- 1 tablespoon apple cider vinegar
- 1 teaspoon garlic powder

Instructions:

1. **Preheat Oven:** Preheat your oven to 325°F (163°C).
2. **Prepare Ham:** Score the surface of the ham and place it in a roasting pan.
3. **Make Glaze:** In a bowl, mix red pepper jelly, Dijon mustard, apple cider vinegar, and garlic powder until well combined.
4. **Glaze Ham:** Brush the mixture over the ham.
5. **Bake:** Cover loosely with foil and bake for 1.5 to 2 hours, basting every 30 minutes.
6. **Serve:** Let the ham rest for 15 minutes before slicing. Enjoy warm.

Maple-Cranberry Glazed Ham

Ingredients:

- 1 fully cooked bone-in ham (6-8 lbs)
- 1/2 cup cranberry sauce
- 1/4 cup maple syrup
- 1/4 cup brown sugar
- 1 tablespoon Dijon mustard

Instructions:

1. **Preheat Oven:** Preheat your oven to 325°F (163°C).
2. **Prepare Ham:** Score the surface of the ham and place it in a roasting pan.
3. **Make Glaze:** In a bowl, mix cranberry sauce, maple syrup, brown sugar, and Dijon mustard until smooth.
4. **Glaze Ham:** Brush the mixture over the ham.
5. **Bake:** Cover loosely with foil and bake for 1.5 to 2 hours, basting every 30 minutes.
6. **Serve:** Allow the ham to rest for 15 minutes before slicing. Enjoy warm.

Citrus and Herb Marinated Ham

Ingredients:

- 1 fully cooked bone-in ham (6-8 lbs)
- 1/2 cup orange juice
- 1/4 cup lemon juice
- 1/4 cup olive oil
- 2 tablespoons fresh rosemary, chopped
- 2 tablespoons fresh thyme, chopped

Instructions:

1. **Preheat Oven:** Preheat your oven to 325°F (163°C).
2. **Prepare Marinade:** In a bowl, combine orange juice, lemon juice, olive oil, rosemary, and thyme.
3. **Marinate Ham:** Score the surface of the ham and brush with marinade. Let it marinate for at least 2 hours, or overnight in the refrigerator.
4. **Bake:** Place the ham in a roasting pan and cover loosely with foil. Bake for 1.5 to 2 hours, basting every 30 minutes.
5. **Serve:** Let the ham rest for 15 minutes before slicing. Enjoy warm.

Honey-Cider Glazed Ham

Ingredients:

- 1 fully cooked bone-in ham (6-8 lbs)
- 1/2 cup honey
- 1/4 cup apple cider
- 1/4 cup brown sugar
- 1 tablespoon Dijon mustard

Instructions:

1. **Preheat Oven:** Preheat your oven to 325°F (163°C).
2. **Prepare Ham:** Score the surface of the ham and place it in a roasting pan.
3. **Make Glaze:** In a bowl, mix honey, apple cider, brown sugar, and Dijon mustard until smooth.
4. **Glaze Ham:** Brush the mixture over the ham.
5. **Bake:** Cover loosely with foil and bake for 1.5 to 2 hours, basting every 30 minutes.
6. **Serve:** Allow the ham to rest for 15 minutes before slicing. Enjoy warm.

Blackberry Glazed Ham

Ingredients:

- 1 fully cooked bone-in ham (6-8 lbs)
- 1/2 cup blackberry preserves
- 1/4 cup balsamic vinegar
- 1/4 cup brown sugar
- 1 tablespoon Dijon mustard

Instructions:

1. **Preheat Oven:** Preheat your oven to 325°F (163°C).
2. **Prepare Ham:** Score the surface of the ham and place it in a roasting pan.
3. **Make Glaze:** In a bowl, mix blackberry preserves, balsamic vinegar, brown sugar, and Dijon mustard until smooth.
4. **Glaze Ham:** Brush the mixture over the ham.
5. **Bake:** Cover loosely with foil and bake for 1.5 to 2 hours, basting every 30 minutes.
6. **Serve:** Let the ham rest for 15 minutes before slicing. Enjoy warm.

Garlic and Honey Glazed Ham

Ingredients:

- 1 fully cooked bone-in ham (6-8 lbs)
- 1/2 cup honey
- 6 cloves garlic, minced
- 1/4 cup soy sauce
- 1 tablespoon Dijon mustard
- 1 teaspoon black pepper

Instructions:

1. **Preheat Oven:** Preheat your oven to 325°F (163°C).
2. **Prepare Ham:** Score the surface of the ham and place it in a roasting pan.
3. **Make Glaze:** In a bowl, mix honey, minced garlic, soy sauce, Dijon mustard, and black pepper until well combined.
4. **Glaze Ham:** Brush the mixture over the ham.
5. **Bake:** Cover loosely with foil and bake for 1.5 to 2 hours, basting every 30 minutes.
6. **Serve:** Allow the ham to rest for 15 minutes before slicing. Enjoy warm.

Lemon-Herb Glazed Ham

Ingredients:

- 1 fully cooked bone-in ham (6-8 lbs)
- 1/2 cup lemon juice
- 1/4 cup olive oil
- 1/4 cup honey
- 2 tablespoons fresh thyme, chopped
- 2 tablespoons fresh rosemary, chopped
- Salt and pepper to taste

Instructions:

1. **Preheat Oven:** Preheat your oven to 325°F (163°C).
2. **Prepare Ham:** Score the surface of the ham and place it in a roasting pan.
3. **Make Glaze:** In a bowl, combine lemon juice, olive oil, honey, thyme, rosemary, salt, and pepper. Whisk until well mixed.
4. **Glaze Ham:** Brush the mixture over the ham.
5. **Bake:** Cover loosely with foil and bake for 1.5 to 2 hours, basting every 30 minutes.
6. **Serve:** Let the ham rest for 15 minutes before slicing. Enjoy warm.

www.ingramcontent.com/pod-product-compliance
Lightning Source LLC
LaVergne TN
LVHW061956070526
838199LV00060B/4147